HUMANS OF BALLOU

HUMANS OF BALLOU

THE BALLOU STORY PROJECT

VOLUME 3

Published by
Shout Mouse Press, Inc.
www.shoutmousepress.org

Copyright © 2016 Shout Mouse Press, Inc.
ISBN-13: 978-1945434006 (Shout Mouse Press, Inc.)
ISBN-10: 1945434007

Photography produced in partnership with Lana Wong / Shootback Project,
except when otherwise indicated.

Book Design by Amber Colleran.

This book is dedicated to the inspiring minds of Ballou,
the ones who work in unity to make this school a home.

Contents

Preface

Our third volume of The Ballou Story Project, *Humans of Ballou,* was inspired by the photo blog sensation "Humans of New York" in one key way: authenticity.

What Brandon Stanton, the photographer behind "Humans of New York," tapped into when he started taking photographs of strangers on the streets of New York was our need for authentic connection to the people arounds us. Our need to move beyond assumptions or false veneers. Our need to not feel alone.

Authenticity is that key to connection. And authenticity requires courage, humility, reflection, and grace. The authentic photograph may not be you at your most glamorous, but it is you at your most real. Likewise, the authentic stories we tell about ourselves are not always triumphant. But it is that unfiltered reveal of your truest self — of your hopes, regrets, hard lessons, big dreams — that reminds us that in our remarkable diversity, we are connected. We are all gloriously — and merely — human.

In seeking to capture the real *Humans of Ballou*

in writing, we challenged students to first and foremost 'Be Real.' "Be real," instructions read, "like you're up talking to your best friend late at night. That kind of real. Could be serious. Could be light. Just be sure it's totally you." Some students chose to edit something from their voice-driven personal statements that we had helped them write earlier in the year. Others chose to compose something entirely new, either via self-interview or in conversation with another. We asked them to seek out the questions that revealed sides of themselves that perhaps others didn't know, to communicate their essence. For example:

Tell us about a big turning point in your life (good or bad).

What do you believe in? What are you afraid of?

Tell us about something you miss (from childhood, or from last year, or from yesterday...)

Tell us about something or someone that you love.

What motivates you to do as you do?

What's a hard lesson you've learned? How did you learn it?

Why is it good to be you?

And the responses we got were heart-felt and sometimes heart-breaking, with writers sharing moments and memories that came alive on the page. To express their truest selves, students told stories about the joy of helping others, the struggle of fitting in, the pain of losing loved ones, the determination of getting ahead. They emanated confidence or confessed being shy. They talked about mistakes. They talked about pride. In every case, we left these writing sessions with not only a deeper sense of the person behind the pen, but of the bridges we build through the act of sharing and listening, without judgment.

Once students had finished their own conversations with the page, they took that same attitude of openness to speak to some of the adults at Ballou who help to make this school a home. Their goal was to come up with their own questions and to understand: *Who are you outside of these walls? What brought you here, and why do you do what you do? How can we know you as just another human, making your way?*

As you'll see in the pages that follow, both Ballou students and Ballou adults took this mission to heart. Through their candid commentary we learn not only about what motivates these adults to support the youth who need it most, but also about themselves as daughters losing fathers, as friends losing friends, as young people making mistakes, rethinking priorities, and changing their lives. It's clear from these conversations not only how comfortable these students and educators are with being real, but how genuine are their relationships, their commitments to knowing each other not just casually but well.

Finally, pictures communicate what words alone — even these poignant words — cannot. We depended upon the talents of student photographers to capture or contribute images that revealed their truest selves and those of their partners in conversation. Students snapped photos in the classrooms and hallways of

Ballou, and also took a photo field trip to capture context — from metro stops to middle schools to monuments to museums — communicating not just who they are but where they come from, both East of the River and along the National Mall. These young people are both of iconic Washington, DC and outside it, straddling two worlds and staking their claim: "This is our city, where we belong." The result is a collection of portraits that builds bridges. As student photographer, Shahid Daniels, says, "When you take a portrait, you really see that person's soul. You feed off their energy. You feel for that person in a way that's different, that's deep."

We cannot underestimate the power of that connection, the importance of that uncovering. This is true not only for participants of the project, but for all who read this book. The Ballou Story Project series has always been a chance for Ballou to tell its own story about Ballou, and in doing so, these writers are telling a story that often goes unheard. Many do not know these true selves. Many assume they know without listening. These assumptions can weigh heavy, but they can also provide motivation to surpass and succeed. It is our hope that with this collection, these *Humans of Ballou* engender the joy and inspiration and respect they deserve, and that through their example we can continue to build community and connection, one conversation at a time, and with each turn of the page.

—KATHY CRUTCHER
EDITOR, SHOUT MOUSE PRESS

Being a photographer is way out of the element of Southeast Washington, DC. Most of the people here, they want to be a basketball player, or football player, or even do things that aren't right, but for me **photography is my outlet.** It expresses my emotions, and really expresses me personally. It brings you into my life and things that are going on around me.

Photography is like therapy. It's therapeutic. Once you get that right image, it's like when you hit a buzzer beater shot as a basketball player. There's no feeling like it.

I like to shoot organically. I don't like to pose. And I love doing portraits. A picture can speak a thousand words, you know. It never says just one thing to anybody. And **when you take a portrait, you really see that person's soul.** You feed off their energy. You feel for that person in a way that's different, that's deep.

—SHAHID DANIELS

Modeling is about confidence. Normally I'm very shy. You know Cancers, they are SHY. I used to think I couldn't do a lot of stuff, like I didn't have a talent. But after my first modeling show, I realized getting up in front of people is not that bad. **My heart would be pounding,** but I don't even get scared no more. I think, *OK, Showtime. Let's do this!* Now I love it.

When I model I feel a lot of things. I feel good about myself. I feel like I'm accomplishing something. And **I'm more brave. I feel like I can try new things.** I know now it's not bad to try new things, because it might end up being your passion.

—ASHLEY BOYKIN

I remember the day that I transitioned from being a boy to being a young man. It was the day I got the Achievers Scholarship. It showed me that **hard work really pays off, but the process isn't always easy.**

I wrote four essays for the Achievers Scholarship — a $62,000 scholarship for college. But when I was ready to turn in my application, I couldn't find my essays. I couldn't find them at home or in my locker. I told my teacher who told me to start over. At that point, I was like, *I might as well forget it.*

Two days later, I decided I shouldn't let this chance go by. I believe that **if you aspire to do great you'll see failure as an opportunity to be creative and try again.** So I wrote the four essays over, and they were better than the first four because this time I really thought about what I was doing. I learned that **I need to put 100% effort into everything I do** because I might not always have a second chance to prove myself like I did this time.

I also learned if I set my mind to do something, nothing will stop me. That is exactly what my motive was when I rewrote my essays. **I was determined, I had a goal, and I worked hard to achieve it.** All of the characteristics of a man.

—TAJUAN BOOMER

I spent my beginning years of life in a very small circle in the state of Ohio. When I decided to move to Washington, DC, I had no job. I packed two boxes of clothes and a couple of keepsakes and mementos. I drove seven hours to DC, slept on friends' couches for six months, and I crossed my fingers that I would find a job somewhere. I was lucky enough to be offered a job at Ballou, which was probably one of the greatest decisions that I've ever made. It has been one of the most challenging life experiences, and I absolutely would not change it for the world. **I love this city, this school, the staff, and most of all, the students.**

Sometimes the outside world sees [my students] as one type of person, **but I get to see them in a different light.** They see them as kids who get into trouble, kids who don't care about things, who don't care about their future, about their community. I'm lucky enough that I get to be in a position where I get to see the deeper side of them and see all the great goals that they have for themselves. I get to see the little things. I get to see them in the hallway with friends. I get to watch them stick up for me when they've only known me for six months and be supportive and protective. I see them struggle and face challenges and somehow overcome them. Maybe not at first, maybe it takes a couple of tries for them. Maybe they get frustrated and they leave and then have to come back and try again. But **so many of my students don't give up even when they feel like it, and I think that is such an inspiration.**

—MS. BERNARDO,
IN CONVERSATION WITH
LITZI VALDIVIA-CAZZOL

What makes you motivated to stay ranked in your class?

My family, my parents. We're from Bolivia. Bolivia and here, in America, they have different systems of education. Some kids don't even go to school there.

What do you want to do when you finish school?

I want to major in early education and teach. It's my third year working with Reach, which is a corporation, and we tutor little kids. A while ago I realized how I really put a lot of time and effort into [this work], and so I want to put more time and effort into it.

What do you hope for for the kids you work with?

That they continue to do well, because I think they have people telling them that they can't do this or that. I'm just patient with them, just telling them, you know, you can do what you want. And I guess they're starting to actually realize that they can do what they want. I hope they take that with them no matter who says what to them.

What do you tell yourself to keep you motivated?

I just remind myself of my accomplishments. I don't really like saying I did this or that, like I'm better than people. I don't know. I just realize that at the end of the day, if I'm not doing so good, I know other people are doing worse. So I can get passed it. Deal with it.

What's been the happiest moment of your life so far?

Realizing I wanted to become a teacher. Just being assured that being a teacher is the path that I want for myself. I mean, if I have made a difference in a child's life already, I know I can make another impact. I want to do work that will better the future of children, to let them recognize they have so much potential at a young age, because it took me a while to realize that, too. That just made me really happy, that I knew who I wanted to be.

—LITZI VALDIVIA-CAZZOL

What is something you really want people to know about you and why?

What I want everyone to know — you, my students, my boss, my wife, my family — is that I really do care about what I'm doing, about everything I do. **I really care about teaching, about being a good husband,** being a good... whatever I'm trying to be. I really do try and think about it and work hard even though sometimes I fail.

What is something about being a teacher that you didn't realize but then started to understand?

Every student needs something different, and usually something very different. That's what I love about teaching. The students, like you, who are high achievers and ready to go to Harvard — the things you need are very different. You need a push to go even higher, like college application recommendations. And then other students need to find a way to sit down without throwing desks. That's on the other end. **I'm trying to figure out how to help all my students better.**

I feel like teaching history is a small part of my job and the biggest part is figuring out how to reach each student. I feel like teaching is more psychology than most people realize. Trying to read people. Figuring out what they most need and how I can best meet that need.

—MR. FABER,
IN CONVERSATION WITH DIANE YOMKIL

I take school very seriously because I'm in this country full of opportunities. I came from Cameroon, where things are very different, especially at school. In Cameroon, the teacher doesn't have time to explain the lesson, like they do here. We don't always have necessary materials either, like computers or books, to learn for a test or do a project. It's hard to have good grades, or do well in school. So in 9th grade in Cameroon, my grades were not that good. But when I came here, the teachers took time to help me, and to explain things to me. They even stayed after school to help me understand. Also here with computers, internet, books, I have less difficulties to learn and study.

I'm proud that in one year I'm the first 11th grade student with a GPA of 4.3. And I'm proud of all the certificates that I've earned due to my hard work. I'm proud of that.

Coming here showed me how lucky I am and that I have to do my best to honor my family and to succeed. I don't want to play with my future. I want to be a lawyer. I want to fight injustice. When I was in Cameroon, I wanted to be a doctor to fight disease and help my family. But when I moved here and I heard about everything that was happening — the shootings, and what happened with Michael Brown and Freddie Gray, I just feel like somebody — maybe I! — need to do something. Somebody needs to make a change.

—DIANE YOMKIL

How did you overcome that?

Changing my environment really helped. I wasn't 100% happy with where I was in college, so I decided to transfer to New Orleans where my mom was. And in time I kind of healed. Like some of the sadness and some of the issues I had with their death...it just got better. One day at a time.

And what's the most important thing you've learned as a principal?

Well I learned when I was a teacher that when you have relationships with people, students, parents, staff...that's really important to the work. And when they know you really love and care for them, that's the first step. I feel like now that the students see me as someone who really cares, they're responding differently, because they know that at the end of the day I really care about their learning and experience and I want this place to be a safe school that you guys love. I think making sure people feel deeply loved is really important.

—DR. REEVES,
IN CONVERSATION WITH DIANE YOMKIL

What is the hardest thing you had to overcome?

When I was a freshman in college, I went to Spelman for two years. I moved from California to Atlanta. During my freshman year, two of my friends from California were murdered while I was in school. It was really difficult for me to be away from my family. This was the first time I had known anyone who had been murdered. I had known people who had died, but this was really tragic. One of them was a very violent murder. So it was really hard dealing with that being 18, 19. That was the hardest thing I've dealt with for sure.

I look up to my mother because although she is 54 years of age, she is in college trying to better herself. While in college, she has a steady job with good benefits. She works with people who have mental health issues and still she comes home and takes care of our family every day. She's always wanted to improve her education. **I am extremely proud of my mom because she followed her heart.** She didn't give up on herself, even during hard times in her life.

—CARMELA PENDLETON

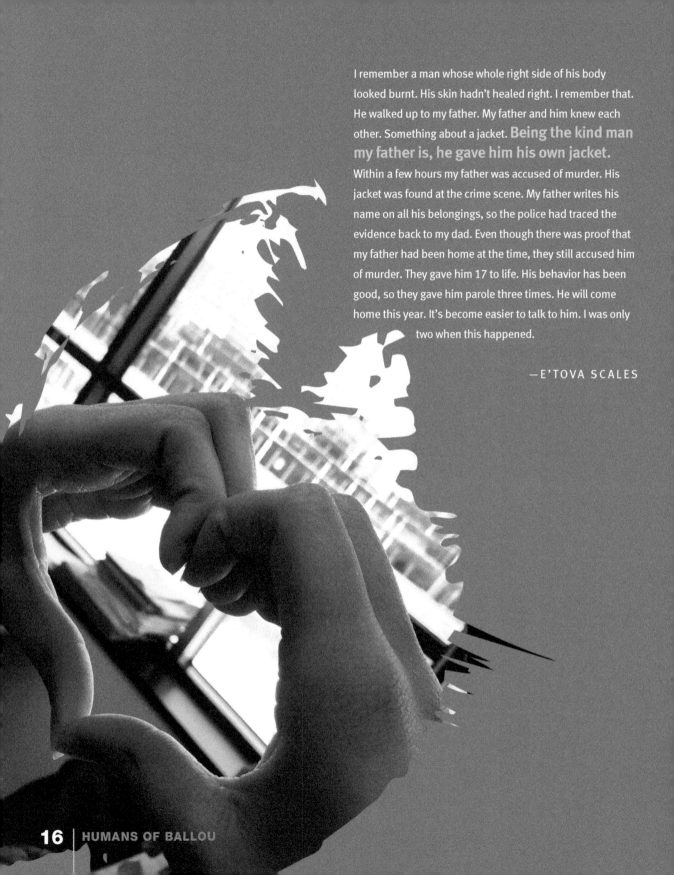

I remember a man whose whole right side of his body looked burnt. His skin hadn't healed right. I remember that. He walked up to my father. My father and him knew each other. Something about a jacket. **Being the kind man my father is, he gave him his own jacket.** Within a few hours my father was accused of murder. His jacket was found at the crime scene. My father writes his name on all his belongings, so the police had traced the evidence back to my dad. Even though there was proof that my father had been home at the time, they still accused him of murder. They gave him 17 to life. His behavior has been good, so they gave him parole three times. He will come home this year. It's become easier to talk to him. I was only two when this happened.

—E'TOVA SCALES

There's something about taking a picture. I like being able to say, *I took that*. Plus I like seeing smiles on people's faces. I like taking pictures of people being carefree, having a good time. I like to capture moments like that.

Why are those moments important?

It can show us that we can actually be happy, and we don't always have to worry about the painful moments in life. I want to build a website that will keep these memories in store so they'll never be forgotten.

—JOSEPHINE JACKSON

What do you hope for?

To go to college and do the best I can so I can become a chef.

When you become a chef, what is one of the first things you are going to cook?

The first thing I want to cook is probably some soup, but not for me, my mom, or my family. It would be for a homeless shelter because when I see old people, my heart melts, and to see them, or any people, in hot weather, cold weather, with nowhere to go, and no one is helping them, I think about how everyone else gets to go home and eat and sleep, but no one is caring for them in the streets... The shelters get closed early in the morning and they're outside until like 6:00, 7:00 at night, and they're cold because it's cold, so I want to give them some soup to warm them up.

Sharing food with people is special. It's a way I'll be able to give back and help my community. I feel as though I am really blessed, and I am trying to live my life right.

What made you want to be a chef?

When I was five years old my dad passed away. He didn't go to culinary school, but he got training and a certificate and he worked at Ruby Tuesday. He passed away from lung cancer. I knew he was a chef, and it wasn't like I wanted to be a chef because he was a chef, but when I was twelve I was watching the Food Channel and I was like, *this stuff is really good*. And then thinking back I was like, *my father was a chef*. And that's what he did — he would please people. He would bring food from his job home, trays and stuff. And that's what I want to do. Not only give back to my family but to other people, too.

—CHANTELLE MORGAN

A big turning point was when I left corporate America and moved over into the Ballou community. I decided, instead of chasing my career goals and finances, to pretty much live for myself. I decided **I wanted to get more involved in the community and in the lives of youth and see of what benefit I could be.**

That was a big turning point because **it helped me start to value what was really important in life, which to me are people and relationships and experiences.** Back then, it was things, status, access. It was all these different things that are fleeting and temporary and ultimately unfulfilling. But today, I'd rather just be with people than to have things or to be pursuing something temporary.

—MR. TAYLOR,
IN CONVERSATION WITH TAJUAN BOOMER
AND CHANTELLE MORGAN

How have your students impacted your life?

Oh my goodness, **my students are the reason I continue to go on.** Without them, I guess I would be totally clueless about some of the hard and horrible things that are happening to children around the world, so experiencing them daily motivates me to come to school, to give my best, because it's the right thing to do. It's my responsibility.

How do you think your students feel about you being there for them? Because some of them may not have people to talk to at home, so how do you think you play a role in their life?

I definitely think that it's a love-hate relationship. When they come to me, they know that I'm going to be real... I'm a keep-it-real teacher. I don't mince my words, **I give them the hard facts about their reality, but I also show them how to navigate through it.** I'm going to be consistent. I'm not going to make it easy for you, but years from now, you're going to definitely appreciate my being stern and consistent, and ultimately, loving.

—MS. YARBROUGH,
IN CONVERSATION WITH KAIYA BURNETT
AND CARMELA PENDLETON

My mother is my rock. She is my support, my encourager, my heart. My mother is an amazing, intelligent, wonderful, powerful, and phenomenal black woman. My mother has had a roller coaster life. My mother works hard at anything she does.

My mother is all of the these words above because at 44 years old she has a steady job making good money. She comes home and takes care of the family. After long hours of work — and this is what I am most proud of — she has taken it upon herself to further her education.

My mother has always wanted to continue her journey in college. Now this is her senior year. She should graduate this summer.

I am extremely proud of my mother. She is achieving one of her life goals, and that makes me exceedingly happy.

—KAIYA BURNETT

My style...

...is what I would call articulate. I have like this spice, but I make everything nice. I have confidence in myself as far as what I put on, and when I have confidence in myself, I don't care what anybody else thinks. That's what makes me try new things. I don't even have to talk for you to know my swag. It just shows as I walk through the door.

—KAMARI BLAKNEY

Tell me about something you miss.

I miss old cartoons, like Teen Titans. It was nice to have back in the day. **I miss the old days.**

What do you miss about the old days?

I miss being young, free. I felt more connected then, to family. My brother and I used to watch Dragon Ball Z together. The good one not the bad one. We bonded. We had love for the show, for the action. But the cartoons have changed.

Everything's changed.

—RANDY SAMS

I grew up watching Bruce Lee and his sensei Yip Man. They motivated me a lot. They wanted to make a difference for their country and stop all the stereotypes about their culture and stuff. They trained 100%. They gave it their all and **they never gave up even when it was tough,** and that motivated me.

—REPHAEL SCOTT

I'm not from DC. I was born in Ohio and then lived in Michigan for a big part of my childhood. I feel like living there, I would have grown up differently. Me moving to the DMV, it changed a lot of things.

When I lived in Michigan, I didn't go to a predominantly black school, so that was a huge culture shock for me coming to Ballou. I was used to being around different cultures, different people. I had a lot of hispanic and white friends, and now I have mainly black friends. So at first it felt like I was the outsider, even though I was with people of my kind.

Now I'm used to it, and I'm more comfortable. It's just different, but it's good. When I go to college, I want to go to an HBCU. I like the idea of a predominantly black education. I enjoy it. I find pride in it. It's community.

I still feel like I'm different from people, but I mean, people fit into different places. I fit in with my group of friends, sports teams, people that I have stuff in common with. That's where I fit in. And maybe people aren't meant to fit in with everybody. That's what makes us unique.

—SAMIRAH FESTER-HARRIS

What do you miss?

I miss college. I graduated, but I miss living on campus, and basically living the college life. It's different from the real world. Some things are just optional, whereas in the real world, some things are required. No option. No choices. You just have to do.

—MS. JACKSON,
IN CONVERSATION WITH
DARNE'SHA WALKER

I feel proud about writing three books before I get out of high school. My first book came out when I was like 14, and that's not something a lot of people get to do. It's very exciting!

The first story I wrote was about my grandmother when she was going through breast cancer. She had wanted to write a book about her experience — like, she first started writing a book in her journal — but she wasn't able to actually get it published. So **I thought I could help her.** I wrote the book from my perspective.

When I was asking her about her experiences [to research the story] she was like, "Why you keep asking me about it?" And I was like, "I need to know. I'm putting it in the book!" She kept asking me, "What book, what book?! I need to see some papers." I was kinda keeping it a secret, so I just kept saying, "The book! The book!"

When I told her about the book launch, she was like, "Book launch? You mean you really did put it in a book?!" And I was like, "Yeah! That's what I was telling you!"

So she got all dressed up for the book release. When I read my story, she was crying. I had the whole entire room crying. Everyone was in tears. I was trying not to cry because she was right in front of me. The teachers was crying. Everyone. It was so much. I'm like, *Everyone is so sensitive.* But also, it felt amazing. They were all happy tears. **I felt like I accomplished something big. Something unexpected.**

—DARNE'SHA WALKER

I was here, in DC, when my dad passed away.

My dad was an incredible dad. My mom died when I was three giving birth to my little sister, so he became Mom and Dad for a long time, until he married my second mom who raised me.

So, when I decided after college that I wanted to live here, it was my dad who drove me from Miami to DC — a 17-hour car ride. And when we were in the car, right when we got in, he started crying. I looked at him and said, "Dad, what's wrong?" He said, "I know you're not coming back here. You're going to love DC and you're going to live there." I said, "Well, okay, calm down. We still have a 17-hour drive ahead."

When I moved to DC it felt kind of surreal because it was something I always wanted to do and it was a place I always loved. The first time I went to DC, we were on a family road trip from Miami to New York for a wedding. When we got to DC, it was nighttime and everyone in the car was asleep. My dad said, "Is anyone else awake?" I said, "I am." He and I went outside and we saw the Capitol lit at night and it was beautiful and I said, **"Dad, one day, I'm going to live here."**

So, six months after I had moved, I got a phone call from my older sister who said, "He's not breathing... he's not gone. We're on the way to hospital. You need to come home." I started calling the different airline companies trying to get a flight home. There was a blizzard that was coming to DC. And as I was trying to figure all this out, I got another phone call from my sister who said, "Sha, he's in heaven now."

I dropped to my knees. I said, "No, no, no. He's supposed to give me away at my wedding, he's not gone." Then I asked if they tried to resurrect him. I know it sounds crazy, but I said, "Put me on speaker, I'll try to resurrect him." Obviously he didn't resurrect. It was shocking. **I got on a flight home and had to make sense of my life.**

I grieved by having the best funeral service I could have for him. It was a beautiful, beautiful ceremony. Over 500 people were there. It was awesome. But afterwards what was hard was, "Do I go back to DC? Do I stay in Miami?" My mom said to me, "You know, your dad was so proud of you for being in DC. You know you have to go back." I will forever be grateful for her saying that. If she hadn't said that to me, if she would have said the opposite, which was "I need you here," I would have quit my job, and I probably wouldn't be here right now. Even though she did need me, **she said what I needed to hear, not what she needed at the moment,** and I think that's such a beautiful example of selfless love.

—MRS. CARTAGENA,
IN CONVERSATION WITH
SAMIRAH FESTER-HARRIS

Death is one of those unfortunate situations that just robs us from our loved ones. But before I do things, I sit and think, *Would my father want me to do that? Would he be proud of what I'm about to do?* That's why I just relax myself and always try to better myself. Without [losing him], I wouldn't be as mature and wouldn't be trying to be more responsible. I think that I've come a long way, but there's always room for improvement.

—LIONEL JONES

Being a dual-enrolled student, some people don't always take me seriously. Like they don't really believe that I have the knowledge to pass my classes at Trinity College because sometimes I struggle with my classes here at Ballou.

But they don't know the effort I put into studying, like how hard I try to improve myself. They just look at me like, *Oh these are the people you hang around... They don't know all the work I put in.*

And why do you put in so much work? Why did you decide to enroll in college while finishing high school?

Because I got goals in life. I feel like **you get out of life what you put in,** so if I work hard now, and do my best now while I'm young, once I get older I can relax and chill a little. I can live life the way that I want to. **Why not work hard now for that better future?**

—KENYA HENRY

A turning point in my life was my first semester at VCU when I earned, I think, four Fs and two Ds. My grandfather was in a position to pay for me to go to college and he sat down and had a conversation with us. I remember his exact words: **"The world doesn't owe you anything and neither do I."** With that being said, he was all for education and funding it, but he told me that if I messed up that would be it. I didn't believe him, so I went and partied. Had fun. I mean it was my first year out of the house, first year out of the reign of control and curfews, and **I messed up big time.** He made me pay back some of the money from that semester, and that was what made me turn around.

—MS. MAYO,
IN CONVERSATION WITH ANA SANCHEZ

What's a hard lesson you've learned?

I learned that obviously there are some people in your life that will always be there for you, but that doesn't mean you should take advantage of that. You should always rise to the expectations that they have for you, or at least try your best. Sometime you try to procrastinate or put things off, and it ruins the trust people have in you. It's hard to earn that back.

That's deep. How did you learn that?

So, [over the past few years], I abused a lot of my mom's trust and the expectations that she had for me, and that I had for myself. I put those to the side and forgot what my overall goals were. At one point she said, *If you don't change, I'm not going to trust you anymore.*

My relationship with my mom has always been important to me. I realized I was hurting her as much as I was hurting myself and my future. Her love for me really showed me my value and potential. I didn't want to waste that.

—ANA SANCHEZ

WE ARE BALLOU

What about the community makes you want to stay, or to influence students to do better?

I grew up in the community, so when I go to the area grocery store or walk down the street, I'm constantly saying "Hey," or someone's stopping me just to talk and chat. So **I have an investment in the community by being a part of it.** I moved over here when I was in the 6th grade, and I've always had ties to Southeast and Ballou. **I love it, I treasure it, and I know this is where I'm meant to be.**

How do you feel when people on the news or otherwise talk bad about Ballou?

I feel sad and disappointed, but at the same time, **I feel motivated and inspired to change that stereotype.** So when things like that happen, what can I do? What can we do positively to show again the greatness that's here at Ballou? So that's when my wheels start turning, you know. I can't change the world, I can't even change this whole area, but through the band, that's been my focal point of trying to change people's ideas and mindset of Ballou. I hope I've done a good job of that. **I know it's still a struggle, still a challenge, but at the same time, it's my goal.** It's more of an inspiration to me. It motivates me.

What influenced you to stay at Ballou for so many years?

That's a good question. One of the many reasons I stayed at Ballou is to help the students at Ballou — and help the community — realize **the beauty, the talent, the EVERYTHING that is here,** that we offer to the world. Ballou is looked down on as this place in Southeast, but I just want people to realize the greatness that is floating around these hallways.

—MR. WATSON,
IN CONVERSATION WITH KIARA BURNETT

Ever since I was young, I've been hearing stories about how sick I was as a child. My mother always told me stories about different things that happened when I was a baby. She told me that I had lots of eye surgeries to correct my eyesight and that I had two inguinal hernias in my back, and my left lung had collapsed. But still, I grew up able to do the things that the doctors told me I would never do.

Growing up with this information, I knew that working with babies would be my passion. When I go to college I would like to study Neonatology. That's the subspecialty of pediatrics that focuses on the medical care of newborn infants, especially the ill or premature. I've always cared about people less fortunate than me.

I feel that babies are born to have a meaning in this world, and I want to prove that to people who abandon their children. Maybe they are too young and don't have the time, or they don't realize the responsibility they have. But do they realize that some people who grow up without their family can grow up to be depressed? I don't want more children to feel depressed about losing their family or going from foster home to foster home. I want to help prevent that.

Nothing to me is more important than babies.

—KIARA BURNETT

Getting poor grades had a huge affect on me. I was disappointed in myself because I knew I was capable of passing my classes with much higher grades. Having poor grades meant that I could not participate in any extracurricular activities in or outside of school. I felt left out because everyone else who had better grades was enjoying their life and I was not. I felt like a failure. Experiencing those feelings made me realize I needed to get my act together and fix this problem.

I was determined to make every effort to increase my grades and started being more serious about my school work. I began to turn my failure around by reaching out to my teachers for help when I needed it rather than sitting back and failing. If I was not able to seek help from a teacher, I would stay after school to catch up on work. Also, I asked for extra credit work to help bring up my grades. Regardless of how difficult the work was, I remained focused on succeeding at what I was doing. You can't just be a pretty face and not have the education.

—ARIANIA CAIN

I am someone who enjoys life and wants all that he can get out of it. My biggest fear is that I won't be able to experience everything I've ever dreamed of in my lifetime. Unfortunately I know I can't do it all — everybody's gotta die sometime. But that doesn't mean that I should stop trying to get the most possible out of life.

What are some of those things that you hope to experience?

Things people don't usually get to experience. Like, for instance, how I'm going to Costa Rica over the summer. That's definitely something not many people get to experience. Especially people who live, like, a normal life.

Also [I like] just being in nature. There's a river down by where I live, and I go down there and skip rocks and stuff. I walk around in the woods.

Why's it important to you to get out of your usual environment?

It's important because it helps me spiritually and mentally. It helps me see the world in a better place. Doing things like that, it opens my mind. It relieves all the stress and worries of the world. If I'm in a forest or something, I don't have to worry about anything happening to me because of somebody else or because of society — it's just peace of mind.

—CARL BROWN

"Your vibe attracts your tribe."

That's basically like my motto. It's like you are who you hang with. So if you don't have a good vibe that you're giving off, you're not going to attract the people that embody that.

So just be yourself, and everything else will fall in place.

—JOHNNETTA MOORE

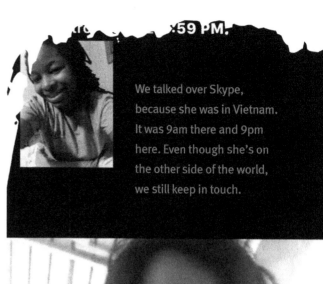

We talked over Skype, because she was in Vietnam. It was 9am there and 9pm here. Even though she's on the other side of the world, we still keep in touch.

What advice would you give to the novice traveler, other than pack lightly?

I'd say finding purpose, that's the biggest thing I'd tell somebody. Don't go somewhere just to see some place. Go somewhere with a goal in mind. Whether the goal is finding the ten craziest foods you can eat or to volunteer or to do something you've never done before. I think if you have a purpose, while you travel, it'll make the travel a lot more meaningful. Volunteering or finding a little job while you're gone is probably the single best thing I've done while traveling. So, find purpose.

—MS. VAKHARIA,
IN CONVERSATION WITH JOHNNETTA MOORE

I have always been a daddy's girl. He's showered me with gifts, and always supported me when I needed him. He motivates me to be successful at anything I try. We have conversations about life itself, and we have a great bond.

One day I was watching the news with my aunt, when I saw a segment about armed robberies in the area. They said, "Two men were arrested after a warrant was served in Southeast. Investigators are trying to determine if these men are the Black Hat Bandits, believed responsible for at least eight armed bank robberies in the D.C. area." I remember these words so clearly as if they were being spoken in real time. Then, I saw my father's mugshot on TV, and underneath it had his name in bold letters.

I couldn't believe that my father, the only man that I could ever picture myself loving, was being profiled as a dangerous bank robber with a deadly weapon.

My father has set me on a certain path. I know who I want to be in life, even though sometimes I feel confused because he's not immediately with me to give that advice. But I visit my father once a month at his prison, and he still acts the same, not like he's in jail. When we're on the phone he talks to me regular, and we're still close. This makes me feel good, but in the back of my head I always think like I'm not going to be able to see him for real for a while.

He always told me that you can't always depend on people being physically there for you, and they may disappoint you. I never thought he would be referring to himself. But even though he's not here right now, his fatherly presence is enough to help me keep going.

—JOHNAY KIBLER

I'm Hispanic. I came to United States to have a better life. But the first day that I came to the United States from the Dominican Republic, it was the *worst* day of my life. I cried because I had never separated myself from my mother and my sisters. My brother and I spent the first week crying and thinking about my mother.

My mother didn't want to cry in front of us when we were in the airport. I used to talk with my friends from the Dominican Republic, and they told me that my mother cried every time that she finished talking to us on the phone.

Every time I heard that, it would break my heart. It made me want to go back, but instead I think about my future and the goals I have made since I came to this country.

My mother always tells me to be an example for the young kids and make a difference in the classroom so they can notice you. The most important thing is always be who you are and not what people want you to be.

—JULEYSSI SANCHEZ

Who has influenced you most in your life and how so?

I come from a small but tight-knit family. One of the biggest inspirations for me as a teacher was always my grandfather. He wasn't college-educated but he knew the history of his hometown forward and backward. People would call him up to get a quote for the newspaper or something like that and he knew everybody, everybody's cousin, all the stories. He was a master storyteller. I realized how much history is tied to our individualized identities, and our family and community identities as well. And **how a good story really had the power to shape people's communities in a positive manner.**

What do you hope for in five years?

That's kind of funny. I've been at Ballou now for five years. And I've seen a world of change that I don't think a lot of the newer teachers, newer staff, and honestly a lot of the newer students have seen. We are in a place now where I can honestly say that our students are getting a high school experience. They are learning, they are going to class. They are writing legitimate research papers and opinion pieces. **We are in a great place right now,** but we are not where we want to be, we are not where we need to be. In five years from now, I just want to see that momentum we've created, that I've been a small part of, and that we as a whole school are a part of — I want to see it going forward. I hope that we don't lose steam, that we keep pushing and keep asking ourselves to be a better school and a better people, **because that's what we're capable of.**

—MR. EVANS,
IN CONVERSATION WITH MARC GASKINS

Yeah, it's easy to get overwhelmed. So why don't you quit?

I want to do better. Because everyone in my family — well some of them went to college, but except for my grandfather, no one graduated — and I want to be the first one my age to actually graduate. I want to start my own business. I want to open a restaurant.

Why a restaurant?

Growing up, me and my mom, we would always watch the Food Network. Especially the show "Chopped." You'd have to figure out how to use random items to make a good dish. I always did stuff like that in the house, using whatever I could find. I didn't time myself or anything, but my mother used to judge the dish.

What's your best creation?

One time I mixed chicken noodle soup and clam chowder and I had seasoned it pretty well. And my mother, she liked it a lot. She loved it. And she doesn't even like chicken!

Will you keep cooking?

Definitely. Now I actually try to focus on making a good meal, a nice dish. And I don't just cook for myself, I cook for my family. It feels good to cook for them, you know?

— MARC GASKINS

So, what makes you happy?

Food, yellow, Minnie Mouse, my family...

Wait, what — Minnie Mouse?!

Yep. She's my favorite character. She's a happy person. She's got Mickey Mouse and Donald and Daisy... She's cool. Not because she's pink, that's not it...

?!?

Ok, it started like this: We went to Disney on Ice one time, and it was me, my dad, and my other three sisters, and he told us all we could get something, and my other sisters got lights. And I was like, "Y'all gonna regret getting them lights, because they're gonna break." So I ended up getting Minnie Mouse. And as years went by, I'm still the only one who has my souvenir. So, you know, **she's been with me. She's been through it ALL with me.** And I still got her.

You still have her?

Oh yeah. She's sitting at home in my treasure chest with my real big big Minnie Mouse, and my yellow Minnie Mouse, and my two little ones, and my Minnie Mouse pajamas... I got a Minnie beach towel...

(Laughing) She like totally became your...

...She's my mascot. Yeah.

—TYANDRA AMES

My mother was diagnosed with breast cancer when we were young. But she still took care of us and gave us everything we needed. She never let that get in the way of anything she had to do. She knew it was killing her, but she didn't let it get in the way of raising her kids.

Ever since then, she's been my role model.

How do you try to live like her?

Every little thing that goes on, school, college, something with my health, I try not to let it get to me. **I try my best to do as she does.** No matter what happened, she still found a way to be our mother and to go to work — through snow, rain, everything. She was just trying to get there. I'm just trying to do the same thing. If something's going on at home, I just get through it, still go to school. I just do what I have to do to become successful.

Does she know how much you love her?

I tell her I love her every day, because you never know when it will be the last day.

She's lucky. You're lucky!

Yeah. It's good to have someone in your house you can look up to. It doesn't have to be someone famous, or someone at the police station, fire station. Doesn't have to be someone with a college degree. It could be someone in your own home. **Your own mother could be your everyday hero.**

—WILLIAM SANDERS

I switched to Ballou Senior High my Sophomore year. I promised my mother that I would get honor roll and make her proud. This was a fresh start. Changing schools was a blessing because my teachers actually helped me out. I had never gotten honors so I was surprised when I got honor roll for the first time. Then I got it the second time, and then I got it the third time, and then this last time. I've gotten honor roll all year round. And this really drove me to do better. Back when I was careless, I said I wanted to go to college but I didn't have a plan. Ballou helped me in preparing for college by telling me about scholarships I could apply to and get opportunities that best fit me.

Now everything has been going according to plan. I have an Achiever's Scholarship, and I am maintaining it. It was a long process. I had to give up my whole summer to earn it, but it was worth it because it gives me better opportunities and chances to go to college.

I want to got to art institutes most of all. I'm mostly into music and fashion. I'm a recording artist, and I love it. I can express myself in a way that I enjoy at the same time. It's something I would love to do and get paid to do. So now, I am not off-task, I am not lazy, I am more engaged in work. I've matured, and I take responsibility for my faults. Now I come on time, I get things done, and do what I have to do.

—DION FOREMAN

One night just a week before school started, I was sleeping, and my mother woke me up. She told me, "Shaun's outside. He was shot."

Immediately I put my clothes on, and I went down there. But when I went, he wasn't there. The policeman said he was alive and went to the hospital. So my mother took me to the hospital and I was thinking he was OK, and that he wasn't in that bad condition. But when we got there, they told us he lost too much blood. He had died on the scene. I felt like the policemen lied to me and he wanted me to feel bad.

Sometimes I don't know how I get through the days without Shaun being by my side. Every day we used to just hang and play ball. Now when I play ball I imagine that he's on the court with me. Sometimes I forget that he's gone and ask people is Shaun home. It makes me feel like he wasn't supposed to die.

Now that he's gone I know that he would want me to experience the things he couldn't. Shaun was a big help in my life. I use his death as a drive because I could have been the one not graduating and becoming a senior this year... The thing that I learned is that pain is a test. A test to make you do two things, which is either to give up or to push harder. In my case, I'm going to push harder and believe in myself so I can be an achiever. Even though there are going to be obstacles, I'm not going to let them stop me from being a successful person. I have a million and one goals I need to reach. Right now, even if Shaun is not physically with me, I know he's assisting me through all hard times.

So many times he said to me, "If I'm not gonna make it, you gotta make it." So I'm not doing this just for myself, I'm also doing it for Shaun.

—DESHON LEGGETT

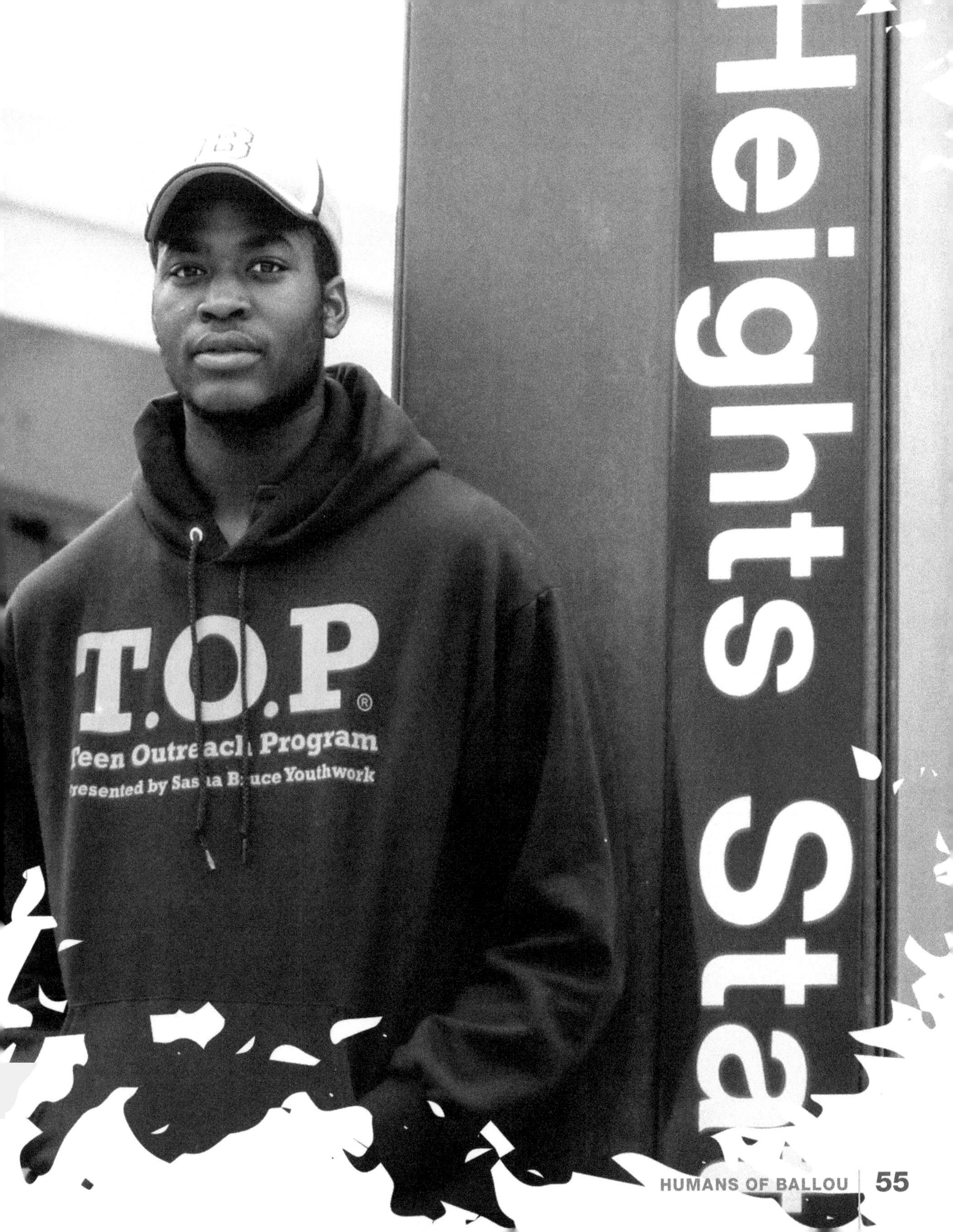
T.O.P
Heights Sta

One of the main reasons for me doing photography is that I want to bring you to my side of town. Most people when they come to DC, what do they see? They see the monuments. The Capitol. Congress. Northwest. They don't get to see the inner city, they don't come down to Southeast, and so nobody sees what's monuments to me. They see Presidents, the White House, and what do I see? I see Southeast. Southeast looks like the Big Chair. It looks like Anacostia Station. It looks like Johnson Middle School, Ballou High School. It looks like the neighborhood I grew up in all my life. It looks like home.

Washington, DC is a beautiful place, and I just want to show people the beauty in Southeast, too. That's my world.

—SHAHID DANIELS

Anacostia Station

Something I miss? I miss my trip to Zambia. Especially the waterfalls. They were something you see out of a movie. You always think that the movies make the scene more... more *something* than what it really is, but when I saw these waterfalls, I realized that this was real — the ability to see your reflection in such clear water. When I looked into that water it was like I could see my whole life in a blink of an eye.

When visiting Zambia I had the chance to connect with others and to experience their culture and learn more about myself in the process. In Zambia I learned how to be calm in the wilderness with monkeys trying to steal our food. I realized that I was taking advantage of the things I had, and I always wanted more and more. I realized what I already have is enough. It helped me be more helpful. It just opened my eyes to see the world is bigger than DC.

—DASHA GOOD

So, tell me about a turning point in your life.

Turning point? Nah, nah, nah. How about this:

'If you could be any comic book character, who would you be?'

I would be Wolverine.

Ha! Ok, how come?

Because he shows durability, resilience, and compassion. **He's a great leader.**

Are you those things?

Yes. **I'm a compassionate person.** I'm not a rebel without a cause. **I'm a peacekeeper.**

—ANONYMOUS

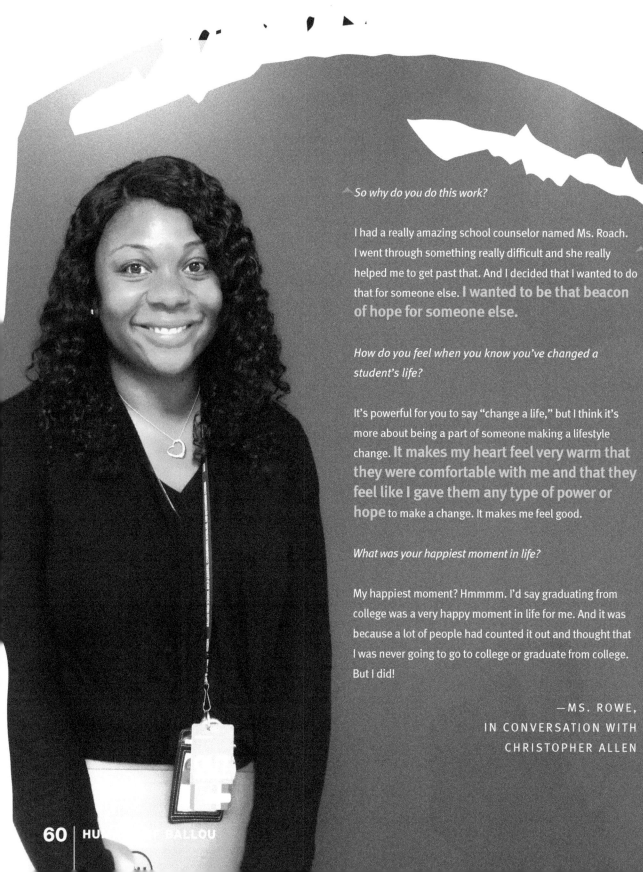

So why do you do this work?

I had a really amazing school counselor named Ms. Roach. I went through something really difficult and she really helped me to get past that. And I decided that I wanted to do that for someone else. **I wanted to be that beacon of hope for someone else.**

How do you feel when you know you've changed a student's life?

It's powerful for you to say "change a life," but I think it's more about being a part of someone making a lifestyle change. **It makes my heart feel very warm that they were comfortable with me and that they feel like I gave them any type of power or hope** to make a change. It makes me feel good.

What was your happiest moment in life?

My happiest moment? Hmmmm. I'd say graduating from college was a very happy moment in life for me. And it was because a lot of people had counted it out and thought that I was never going to go to college or graduate from college. But I did!

—MS. ROWE,
IN CONVERSATION WITH
CHRISTOPHER ALLEN

Writing is a way to relieve stress. It's one way
I use to calm myself down. If you don't feel like talking,
you just put it to pen and paper. I'm proud of my writing
because of the way I put it down. I know it's for me and
no one can take it away.

—CHRISTOPHER ALLEN

I grew up without my father, which was very hard to do. He was shot and killed when I was three years old, so I really don't know much about him. On special occasions like my graduations, birthdays, and parent-teacher conferences, I just wish he was there to say "Good job," give me a hug, or pat me on my back, but he can't. Seeing my other siblings' fathers come around makes me feel depressed and sad because I don't have my father here to talk to about my dreams and aspirations.

Growing up with one parent will help me tell my story, though, because I can help others who might relate. Sometimes your father don't even have to be dead — he could be locked up, or not want to be in your life. You never know what a child is going through. So if I can tell my story, I can help others.

Of all of my mom's kids, I am the only one with my father's last name, "Rose," and I love that because it reminds me that although life can be painful because of the thorns, it's also beautiful because of the blossom.

—DAVEONA ROSE

What makes you you?

My sexy smile. With the chin rub, you gotta add the chin rub. Most people see me every day smiling, and days when I don't smile, everybody thinks there's something wrong, but I'm just naturally happy. For me, when negative things happen, my sense is, it's already done. There's no way to get around it, no way to change it, so just live with it.

I'm used to seeing people get depressed or sad, mainly in school and with my peers and stuff, but **I'm always that one person who would bring out the happiness.**

This attitude is helpful for the career I plan on pursuing: social work. If a person comes in and is sad, I can just be myself and be goofy. Hopefully that will make them feel better about themselves. It works for me.

—IVAN THORNTON

My mom bought me my very own portable radio when I was about seven or six years of age. I would be on the bus singing loud with the headphones in and listening to my favorite radio station. People would look at me and smile and tell me that I had a beautiful voice. I was soon confident in who I was and what I was good at. I was not that shy girl who was getting bullied anymore. I was Destinee Hyman, a future singer and possibly more. I was ready to try new things.

—DESTINEE HYMAN

I play basketball for Ballou. Throughout the season we faced a myriad of obstacles. My coach consistently put her job on the line to protect the team.

One night before we played our rivalry team, Anacostia, my teammates decided to embarrass one of their players on social media by putting up old pictures of them. When game day came and we had our daily talk, Coach told us, "I hope y'all are about to back up all that trash y'all been talking." Everyone seemed to be ready, but our warm-ups showed otherwise. The game went on and we lost by 30 points. The opponent that got embarrassed said, "Actions speak louder than words." We got beat by a team we always blew out until then. It was their first time making it to the playoffs so they came prepared.

I say all this to say that I knew I could have done something differently to help my team... We didn't all take it serious. We thought it was gonna be easy. I let the game slip away just like my teammates. But this situation made me a better and stronger player.

I learned to take responsibility before it's too late.

—AYONNA WILLIAMS

As I was driving I got a phone call. They said, "Hey Andrea, where are you?"

"I'm on my way to my boyfriend's house, it's his birthday."

"Well you may want to come back because our friend group is really hurting right now."

Then they told me that our friend, his name is Victor, he committed suicide. I didn't even know how to react. It was one of those times when I couldn't even say I was devastated immediately because it didn't really register what that meant. No emotion. Nothing registered. I turned around, and I went back.

He had committed suicide early that morning and that night a bunch of us got together and we just prayed. It was really difficult. We prayed for his family, we prayed for his loved ones, we prayed for people who would be affected by the suicide and who would need to be comforted. It was a really traumatic time.

I think something that was really difficult was processing my own emotions. Being self-aware because at first there was no emotion and then there was deep sadness and then honestly, after that, I was really angry with him. That was something I really struggled with because I didn't want to feel angry, and I felt guilty for feeling angry, but I think the anger was coming from a place of *How could you do that? You know there are people who care about you*. Like, *How selfish*. I felt guilty for feeling that way. Finally after being angry, I guess it went back to sadness, but it wasn't a sadness that you feel when things first happen. It was *This is just a sad situation* and there's no *Look at the bright side of the situation*, it was just sad.

Over time the sadness, it has faded. It's not something I think about all the time now, or I wouldn't say it affects me on a daily basis. But a way that it changed me is realizing that you never know what people are going through and you really need to value the relationships that you have. For me, Victor was my friend but I didn't know he was suicidal. A lot of people didn't. In fact, on the outside, he was the one at the football games that would be cheering the loudest, always painted up for the football game. At a party he would always be the hypest one there. I think he exuded so much joy because looking back on it that was just a cover up for the deep clinical depression he was experiencing.

It made me realize that there is a lot more to people than what they wear on the surface, and I need to take the time to ask questions. Especially with people I am close to, making sure I am taking the time to really know them and be intentional. I really want to be a person who cherishes relationships because for this relationship with Victor I didn't see the end coming.

In light of how tragic the situation was, the positive change in me was not taking relationships for granted. And I'm not perfect in it. There are times when I go home to Pennsylvania for the weekend to be with my parents and instead of talking to them I'll be on my phone for a couple of hours. Afterwards I'm like, "Man, what am I doing?" I mean, is it morally wrong? No. But I don't want to practice being disengaged with where I am. So I do catch myself in it sometimes and it has gotten easier to do that, but in the long run it's more fulfilling and more rewarding to invest in relationships instead of taking them for granted.

—MS. MAY,
IN CONVERSATION WITH AYONNA WILLIAMS

HUMANS OF LOU

Afterword

Our feelings are our most genuine paths to knowledge. They are chaotic, sometimes painful, sometimes contradictory, but they come from deep within us. And we must key into those feelings and begin to extrapolate from them, examine them for new ways of understanding our experiences. This is how new visions begin, how we begin to posit a future nourished by the past. This is what I mean by matter following energy, and energy following feeling. Our visions begin with our desires.

—AUDRE LORDE, POET AND SOCIAL JUSTICE ACTIVIST

This is a book of visions.

Deeply felt, a gathering of learned and lived experiences.

This book is kindling for the next chapter of incredible lives.

Stepping onto Ballou's campus for the first time I was, and to this day still am, honored to be invited into the recollecting of these students' and educators' lives. It is a bit difficult for me to write about my experience in a way that feels accurate to my heart. I am struggling to portray how moved I am by their work and the time we spent together composing it. How smart and funny and kind and generous all are to me, an outsider in their school. I am constantly learning from their bold and genuine way of sharing truly intimate stories, as well as their initiative to show up for the occasion of storytelling and writing.

Relative to what these writers were able to accomplish in their essays and interviews, my job as Story Coach was a breeze. Spending time with the writers was often very fun and funny. As coaches and writers, our regular meetings were full of exploration and extrapolation of feelings and experiences. There were times during these quiet moments of bonding through storytelling that a crucial moment would ignite, and the writer would begin to unfurl the story of their lives onto paper. These were emotional, important moments that deserved the utmost respect and attention. For many of the writers, looking forward on their lives meant paying tribute to the family, friends, and community that helped them along their journey. For others, it was about honoring the people and homelands they had to leave behind, but kept in their hearts.

With the making of this book, these young writers took charge. Took charge over the stories told about them, wrote what is truly of them, and because of this are changing societal narratives by being present with a pen and camera. As a

reader, you have read a lot of heartache, but you have also been witness to many powerful aspirations and tales of adventure. In many of these interviews, the adventure is moving away from home for the first time and attending college. It is building the connections to start a business, become a chef, or give back to their families and community that gave to them in times of need. It is reflecting on a life that brought them into education, on the trials and triumphs of having positive, loving impact on youth and your community. The ways in which fear shaped a decision or choice. It is recognizing the tangible effects of hard work and fortitude. Learning from the rough moments. It is honoring people they love and people they lost. It's being silly and wanting to make others feel happy in their presence. The undertone of it all: love and dedication to one's self, community and family, and making right.

For me, *Humans of Ballou* is about talking back to a society that believes it can tell you who you are without your consent. It is reclaiming ground and telling others exactly who you are on your own terms and with your own breath. These writers speak that which is coming from deep within themselves, making way for their desires. They use their voices and igniting energy to make all of our worlds bigger.

—SHEILA MCMULLIN,
STORY COACH,
SHOUT MOUSE PRESS

Acknowledgments

This third volume of the Ballou Story Project could not have been possible without the support of a number of hard-working folks who believed in the importance of empowering these young people to share their stories.

For coordinating these writers every week, we cannot thank enough Ballou teacher Shajena Erazo Cartagena. Ms. Cartagena was the motivating force behind these authors, and she gave selflessly of her time over and over again to make this project happen. She is an

inspiration to her students and to those of us at Shout Mouse Press!

We also thank all the Ballou staff who gave authentically of themselves by taking part in interviews and photo shoots: Dr. Reeves, Mr. Watson, Mr. Evans, Ms. May, Ms. Mayo, Mr. Faber, Ms. Vakharia, Ms. Rowe, Ms. Yarbrough, Ms. Jackson, Ms. Bernardo, and finally Mr. Taylor, who also recruited students and supported during photography and writing sessions. What a tremendous team of supporters at Ballou! Thank you.

For mentoring these writers each week and for serving as project lead, we thank Story Coach Sheila McMullin, who gave generously not only of her time but also of her talents, her empathy, her heart. She and fellow Story Coach Sarai Johnson brought laughter and compassion to these writers, and their investment in building relationships made this book possible. We are lucky to count them members of this team!

For the striking photography throughout this book we thank a team of Ballou student photographers led by Shout Mouse Photo Coach and Shootback founder Lana Wong. During our 'Photo Field Trip,' Lana helped students capture powerful imagery of each other and of their hometown by providing both cameras and mentorship. In particular we thank Ballou student photographer Shahid Daniels, whose striking portraits make clear his promising future ahead as a professional photographer. Likewise, Josephine, Kaiya, and Kiara demonstrated exceptional talent and vision in their work. We wish them and all of these emerging artists the opportunities for growth and success that they deserve.

For the smart graphic design of this book, we thank Amber Colleran, who knew just how to help these stories and images sing. Her professionalism helps these voices get the respect and consideration they deserve, and we are grateful.

None of this work would have been possible without a generous grant from the HMFC fund, for which we are enormously grateful. The folks behind this fund introduced us to Ballou and served as constant encouragement and support.

And most of all we thank these dedicated students who gave up lunch periods and stayed after school, always driven by the power of sharing their story with readers who needed to hear it. The selflessness and courage and ambitions of these authors will stay with us. Writing with — and learning from — these incredible teens was such a gift, and a joy.

—KATHY CRUTCHER
FOUNDER, SHOUT MOUSE PRESS

Photo Credits

The photographs throughout this book come from a variety of sources: Ballou students or Shout Mouse staff on-site at Ballou High School; students or staff during a photo field trip that took us through the neighborhoods East of the River to the National Mall; or, when necessary, provided by students or staff themselves from other photo shoots. When possible, we give credit below to student photographers and to Lana Wong, Shout Mouse Photo Coach. Sometimes students shared cameras; please forgive omissions or errors.

Credits listed by page number.

Chantelle Morgan / Tajuan Boomer: 21, 72
Christopher Allen: 46
Destinee Hyman: cover image of Chris, 46
Diane Yomkil: 12, 14
Johnay Kibler / Samirah Fester-Harris: back cover image of Shahid, 36, 70
Johnnetta Moore: 43, 45, 53, 74
Josephine Jackson: cover image of Deshon, 7, 27, 37, 44
Juleyssi Sanchez: 42, 70
Kaiya Burnett: 20, 21, 39, 56, 66, 73
Kiara Burnett: 23, 38, 56, 57, 80
Lana Wong: cover image of Carl, 25, 36, 41, 48, 56, 58
Litzi Valdivia-Cazzol: cover images of Kaiya and Kiara, 8
Randy Sams: 57
Rephael Scott: 20
Shahid Daniels: 2, 24, 30, 35, 40, 47, 50, 54, 62, 64, 67, 74
Tajuan Boomer: 17, 19
Tyandra Ames: 21

Shahid Daniels would like to dedicate his photography to his uncle, Marcus Robinson.

About Shout Mouse Press

www.shoutmousepress.org

Shout Mouse Press is a writing program and publishing house for unheard voices.

Through writing workshops designed for all levels of literacy, Shout Mouse empowers writers from marginalized communities to tell their own stories in their own voices and, as published authors, to act as agents of change.

Our authors include incarcerated youth, at-risk teens in Washington, DC, and exploited children in Haiti, all of whom are served by mission-aligned partner nonprofits working to provide enrichment and leadership opportunities for their communities.

Shout Mouse authors have produced original children's books, memoir and poetry collections, and novels-in-stories that engage a diverse audience as well as open hearts and minds.

You can find our full catalog of minority-authored, mission-driven books at www.shoutmousepress.org/catalog.

About Shootback

www.shootbackproject.org

Shootback empowers young people to tell their own stories and express their creative voices through photography, writing, and critical thinking about the world around them. Shootback started in Nairobi, Kenya in 1997 by putting cameras in the hands of teens from Mathare, one of Africa's largest slums, and culminated in the publication of *Shootback: Photos by Kids from the Nairobi Slums,* a documentary film, and an international traveling exhibition. Nineteen years on, Shootback continues to train a new generation of young photographers in Nairobi and DC in collaboration with various nonprofit organizations.

Shout Mouse Press is proud to partner with the Shootback team, who coach our authors to produce striking original photography for our books.

We Believe

We believe everyone has a story to tell. We believe everyone has the ability to tell it. We believe by listening to the stories we tell each other — whether true or imagined, of hopes or heartbreaks or fantasies or fears — we are learning empathy, diplomacy, reflection, and grace. We believe we need to see ourselves in the stories we are surrounded by. We believe this is especially true for those who are made to believe that their stories do not matter: the poor or the sick or the marginalized or the battered. We feel lucky to be able to help unearth these stories, and we are passionate about sharing these unheard voices with the world.